WHERE IN THE WORLD IS INDONESIA?

GEOGRAPHY LEARNING

CHILDREN'S EXPLORE THE WORLD BOOKS

BABY PROFESSOR

EDUCATION KIDS

In this book, we're going to talk about the country of Indonesia. So, let's get right to it!

WHERE IS INDONESIA?

Indonesia is part of the continent of Asia and is located in the southeastern section of the continent. It is a huge country. It covers over 1.8 million square kilometers of landmass as well as 93,000 square kilometers of ocean. Its size is a little smaller than three times the size of the state of Texas. Ranked against other countries in terms of landmass, it would be ranked number 15. In fact, Indonesia is so spread out and vast that it takes over 12 hours of flying to get from one side of the country to the other. It covers three different time zones.

Yogyakarta, Java Island Indonesia

Indonesia is composed of over 17,000 islands. It is the largest archipelago, which means group of islands, in the world and is surrounded by the Indian Ocean to the west and the Pacific Ocean to the east. About 1/3 of the islands are inhabited, but the others are not. Java is the world's most populated island. Over 140 million people live there.

Most of the people of Indonesia live on five main islands:

- Sumatra
- Kalimantan, which is the Indonesian section of Borneo
- Sulawesi, formerly called Celebes
- Jawa, also called Java and which has the huge capital city of Jakarta
- Papua, which is the western section of the country of Papua New Guinea

Countryside in Sumatra

WHEN DID INDONESIA BECOME INDEPENDENT?

Indonesia used to be part of the territories belonging to the Netherlands, but they gained their independence in 1949.

HOW MANY PEOPLE LIVE IN INDONESIA?

Over 263 million people live in Indonesia. It has the 4th largest population of all countries worldwide.

WHAT IS THE TERRAIN LIKE IN INDONESIA?

Some of Indonesia's larger islands have some mountainous terrain, but most of the country consists of lowlands. The tallest peak on the islands is the mountain of Puncak Jaya, which has a height of 5,030 meters and is located on the island of New Guinea.

Puncak Jaya

Damage from 2009 earthquake

Because Indonesia stretches out over the tectonic plates between Australia and the Pacific, it is prone to earthquakes. The country experiences one earthquake and several large vibrations every day.

HOW DIVERSE IS THE POPULATION OF INDONESIA?

The country's motto is "Unity in Diversity" and it's true that Indonesia has one of the most diverse populations worldwide. Over 300 different ethnic groups live there and over 750 languages with their various dialects are in use. Bahasa Indonesia is the country's official language. Bahasa Indonesia comes from the language of Malay that was primarily spoken in the Riau islands.

Even though Bahasa Indonesia is the official language, the local peoples still speak the languages that are part of their individual cultures. The government of the country encourages schools to teach about and nurture a respect for the different diverse cultures and languages.

WHICH DIFFERENT ETHNIC GROUPS LIVE IN INDONESIA?

More than 90% of the people living in Indonesia today came from native peoples. In order of population these groups are:

- Javanese, which make up 42% of the population
- Sundanese, which make up 31%
- Malay, which make up 3.7%
- Maduranese, which make up 3.3%

Traditional Javanese wedding couple

Island of Java, Indonesia

The remaining population, about 20% is a mixture of different groups. Most of the Javanese people live on Java Island, but millions have migrated throughout the island group. The island of Java is very densely populated and is one of the most populated landmasses worldwide. In addition to these groups, people of Chinese heritage also live on the islands, as do Indians as well as Arabs.

WHICH RELIGIONS ARE PRACTICED IN INDONESIA?

The majority of the people of Indonesia, about 88%, are Muslim and their religion is Sunni Islam as taught by the Shafi'i school. Over 12.5% of the world's Muslims live in Indonesia. About 10% of the population is composed of Christians—a mixture of Protestants and Roman Catholics. The remaining 2% are composed of Hindus as well as those who practice Confucianism and Buddhism.

Little Muslim worshiper

Bride and groom marrying at a Mosque

Every citizen must register with one of these six religions. Two people with varying religious beliefs are not allowed to marry unless one of them converts to the other's religion.

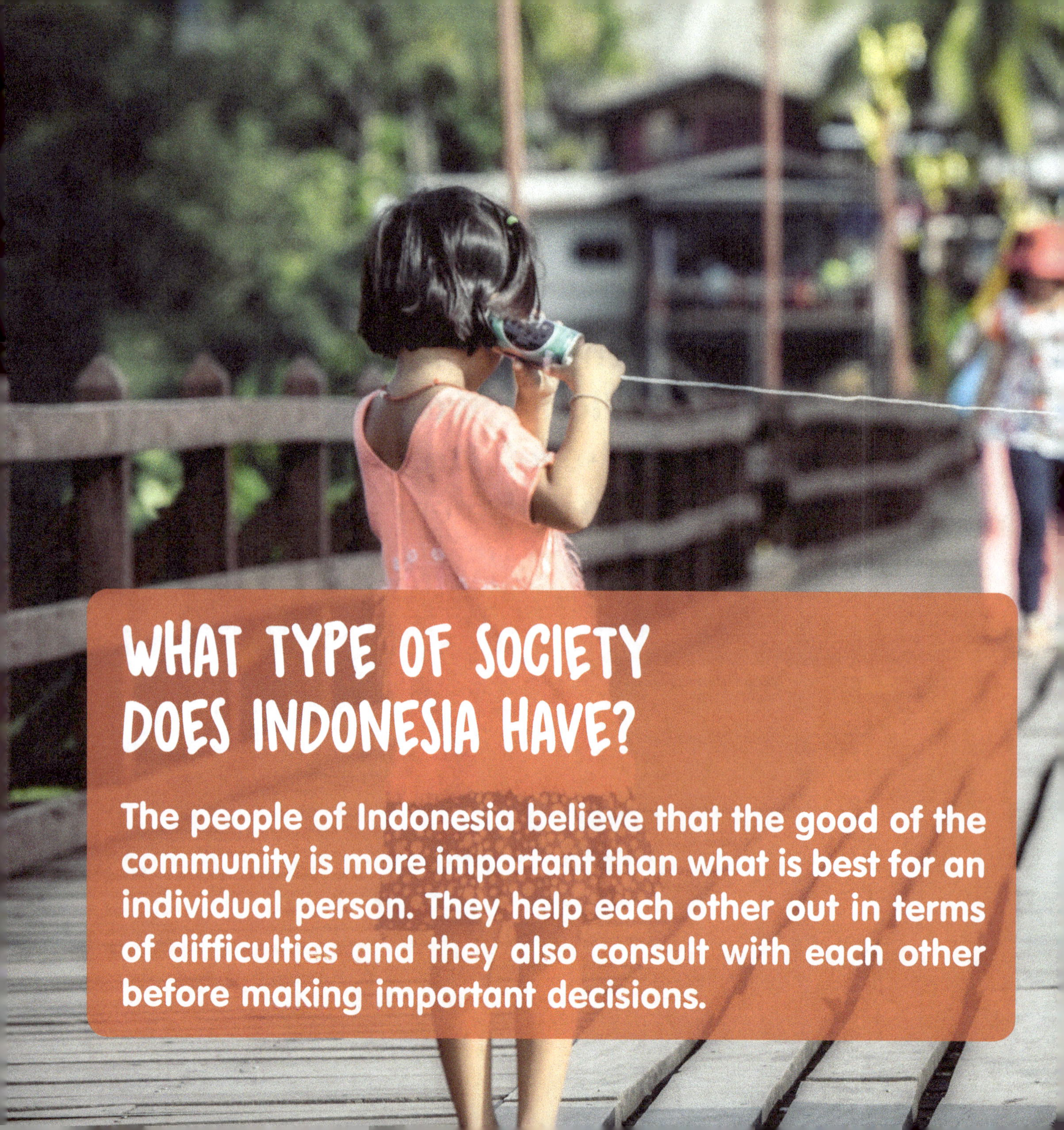

WHAT TYPE OF SOCIETY DOES INDONESIA HAVE?

The people of Indonesia believe that the good of the community is more important than what is best for an individual person. They help each other out in terms of difficulties and they also consult with each other before making important decisions.

Girls talking on a can phone

This culture is seen in every aspect of their daily life and can also be observed in the way they treat their families and extended families. The people form strong bonds with other members within their clans. Although the government doesn't have social security or systems of welfare, the members of a community depend on each other for support when there are problems.

WHAT IS THE HISTORY OF THE COUNTRY OF INDONESIA?

One of the first civilizations to emerge in the country was the naval kingdom of Srivajay. It reached its height of power in the 7th century. The religions of Buddhism as well as Hinduism came to Indonesia during this time period.

Buddhas

Terracotta head of Gajah Mada

The next period of civilization included the Sailendra dynasty, which was ruled by Buddhists, and the Mataram dynasty, which was ruled by Hindus. These dynasties constructed great monuments. During the 13th century, Gajah Mada came to power. He was the ruler of the kingdom of Hindu Majapahit. Under his leadership the kingdom expanded over much of the landmass of Indonesia.

The Europeans arrived in the year 1512 AD. The Portuguese came first. The Dutch came next and they were followed by the British. The Dutch East India Company, which specialized in spices, became the most influential power in the area. They began colonies and took control of the country for several centuries. They referred to the country as the Dutch East Indies and sometimes called it the Malayan Archipelago.

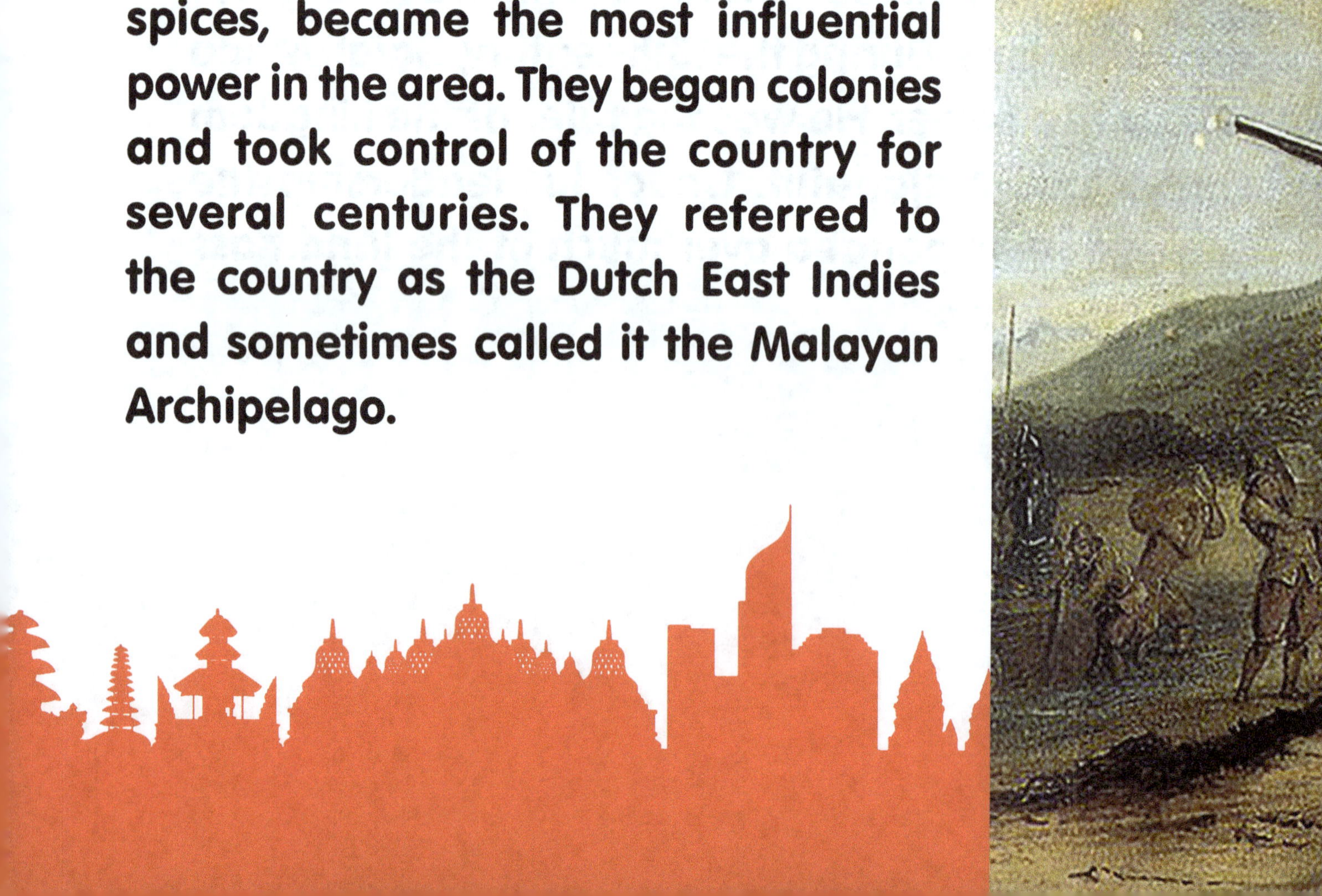

Indus River

The word "Indonesia" was coined by the British and comes from the Greek word for island, which is nesos and the Latin word indus, which means the land situated past the Indus river.

During the Second World War, Japanese soldiers occupied the islands, but after Japan lost and evacuated, Indonesia requested its independence from the Dutch. After several difficult years of struggle, the government of the Netherlands gave Indonesia its independence. Indonesia has had many problems in recent decades.

Beggar

Through 1999, the population was controlled by military rule, which hampered the freedom of the people. The country suffers from poverty as well as overpopulation. Most of the people who live there survive on less than $2 a day.

WHAT NATURAL RESOURCES DOES INDONESIA HAVE?

The country of Indonesia is rich in natural resources. It has vast reserves of oil. It is the only country in southeast Asia that is a member of NATO. It's also the largest producer of palm oil worldwide. Indonesia exports over 3,000 tons of frog legs to the country of France annually.

Palm oil plantation

Asian Palm Civet

Another very strange export is called **kopi luwak**. It is the world's most expensive drink and costs about $1,000 per pound. It's a type of coffee that's transformed by the Asian palm civet, a type of cat-sized mammal related to weasels.

The palm civets eat the coffee berries and then poop them out. After they poop, the berries are collected and sterilized to form the coffee. It sounds disgusting but it's considered to be the best coffee in the world.

Sumatran Tiger

WHAT TYPES OF ANIMALS AND PLANTS LIVE IN INDONESIA?

Indonesia is the second most biodiverse country in the world with Brazil taking the number one position due to the Amazon Basin. Because it is a series of islands, life evolved there in a very different way than in other areas. There are thousands of unique species including:

- The Sumatran tiger, which is endangered and the largest living land mammal that is strictly carnivorous

- The Javan rhinoceros, also known as the Sunda rhinoceros
- The Rafflesia, the world's largest flower, which smells like dung

Rafflesia

Komodo Dragon

Another fascinating animal that lives in the wild only in Indonesia is the Komodo Dragon. This enormous beast with the foul, poisonous breath was discovered by Western scientists in 1910. These fierce hunters eat dead animals, deer, wild pigs, and water buffalos. They will even eat others of their own kind. They have been known to attack and kill humans too.

They are the largest lizards in the world and can get up to 10 feet in length and weigh over 200 pounds. If they bite into an animal and it escapes it won't live for too long. Their saliva has tons of bacteria that will kill its victims within a quick period of 24 hours. The Komodo dragon will follow along until its victim dies and then consume it. The Komodo dragon deserves its dragon name even though it doesn't exhale fire.

Awesome! Now you know more about the country of Indonesia. You can find more Explore the World books from Baby Professor by searching the website of your favorite book retailer.

Visit

BABY PROFESSOR
EDUCATION KIDS

www.BabyProfessorBooks.com

to download Free Baby Professor eBooks
and view our catalog of new and exciting
Children's Books